TOPSY-TURVY

topsy-turvy

charles bernstein

The University of Chicago Press

Chicago and London

The University of Chicago Press, Chicago 60637
The University of Chicago Press, Ltd., London
© 2021 by Charles Bernstein
Published 2021
Printed in the United States of America

30 29 28 27 26 25 24 23 22 21   1 2 3 4 5

ISBN-13: 978-0-226-78360-4 (paper)
ISBN-13: 978-0-226-78374-1 (e-book)
DOI: https://doi.org/10.7208/chicago/9780226783741.001.0001

Library of Congress Cataloging-in-Publication Data

Names: Bernstein, Charles, 1950– author.
Title: Topsy-turvy / Charles Bernstein.
Description: Chicago ; London : The University of Chicago
    Press, 2021. | Includes bibliographical references and index.
Identifiers: LCCN 2020051199 | ISBN 9780226783604
    (paperback) | ISBN 9780226783741 (ebook)
Subjects: LCGFT: Poetry.
Classification: LCC PS3552.E7327 T67 2021 | DDC 811/.54—dc23
LC record available at https://lccn.loc.gov/2020051199

♾ This paper meets the requirements of ANSI/NISO
Z39.48-1992 (Permanence of Paper).

The last—kind words—
I hear'd my—daddy say—
Lord—the last kind words—
I—hear'd my daddy say:

"If I die—if I die—
in the—German war—
I—want you to send my body—
send it—to my mother, Lord.

"If I get killed—if I get killed—
please don't—bury my soul.
I—prof'er just leave me out—
let ya buzzards eat me whole.

"When you see—me comin'—
look 'cross the—rich man's field—
if—I don't bring you flour—
I'll—bring you bolted meal."

I went—to the depot—
I looked up—at the stars—
cried—some train don't come—
there'll be some walkin' done.

My ma—ma—told me—
just before she died—
Lord—precious daughter—
don't you be so wild.

The Missis-sippi river—
you know it's—deep and wide—
I—can stand right here—
see my babe from the other side.

What you do—to me baby—
it never gets outta me—
I—may not see you—
after I cross the deep blue sea.

—Geeshie Wiley

CONTENTS

COGNITIVE
DISSIDENCE

It's no go from the get
go, strumming a mordant
medley from the old days
when we danced with
abandon. Now we are
abandoned, God's
silence deafens us
to each other, and the
fiddlers diddle a
familiar tune. Familiar
and deadly. Wake
up say those still
still small voices:
the Anthrobscene
is playing just north
of here and this is
just a taste of
what's to come.

I'S SONG

after Rückert & Mahler

Comes I to this world abandoned
Having wasted the time I was handed
Till all that's left is the bandage

No matter, unnoticed, time passes
Slowly, as dreams become lashes
Still, alone, caught in rhyme's ashes

Dead to this world's wrong
Dwells, still, I, in my song
In every thorn, at every morn

IF SAPPHO WERE A UFO

And I were a genie
We'd dance on the surface of Pluto
And dine at Ipanema beach in Rio.
Nothing much else
Glues me to this shredded fabric
Of the marvelous, on sale all these years
With no buyers and just three
Authorized sellers. I'd made it almost to
Mars then went home, too much
Mud in those parts, and I missed
The smell of home ground
Even if it turned out to be imported.

September 3, 2017
for John Ashbery

Three steps
ahead, knocked
to floor;
get up,
pushed two
steps behind,
knocked down
again; get
up. Two
steps ahead,
time out.
Pushed back
one step.
Push ahead
three steps,
pushed back
one step,
pushed sideways
five steps.
Knocked out.
Wake up,
groggy, five
steps to
back in
place. Continue
on, as
before, as
after.

ARS POETICA

text
is
wild
er
ness

FREUDIAN SLAP

An old man's best friend
is the past. Aggrievement's

not the end of politics

but a point of contact.
Solidarity of sleights

slips into crystal nights

as compulsory illiberalism's
hypnopompous ardour sours

in the mind's preternatural

larder. Everyday can't be
yesterday since tomorrow is

over before today is done.

You can decide what you
will do but not what you'

ll want. *Fade out*

to the sounds of Shak
Shuka and his Israel / Palestine

Arkestra, coming to you

from the Cosmogonic Ballroom
in midtown Manhattan.

KAREN CARPENTER

Her voice
weeps
sin-
g-
ing
to
God
o-
n a
fre-
quen-
cy
that tu-
nes
out he-
r
cries. We'-
ve
only jus-
t
begun
to fr-
ea-
k—
t-
he
d-
read
l-
on-
ging
to be
cl-

ose
to Y-
ou
wh-
o
tears each soul
to s-
hr-
eds.
Hurting each
other, b-
ut
c-
oming
back f-
or
more.
As i-
f
hurt
is
what
matters.

BEELINE

Bee in my bonnet
Stings all night long
Bee in bonnet
All night long
No sooner morning comes
Begin to holler and bawl

One time I'm in the hen coop
Next at a loading dock
Afraid I'll tumble down the stairs
Then that I may not

Bee in bonnet
Stings night and day
Dozen flights of angels
Not one who knows the way

I'm game if you are
See you on other side
God says he's hiding
Hope to meet her 'fore I die

Bee in my bonnet
Stings me all night long
Dozen flights of angels
Not one'll take me home

PLAN OF ACTION

what if
we just
didn't

Uneven throbs freak
repair, altered by slow
pontoon in sight of sodden
glare. Then, again, my darling
we'll paddle to the pass
where eyes rebuff rough
glances and sins peruse
improbable glances. Once
in time, thrice delayed,
caboose will lead its prey
to inkless odes on feather boats
drunk in nick of fray.

Here it is
Now not there
Gone too soon
Then as was
Just like this
Where I am
Out of sight
Never far
Take me soon
Nearly nigh

If you leave, do it later
Or don't: the history
Of dance crippled by
Riptides, and when that
Passes, this may.

Telling truth is a kind of lying since
Every truth conceals both other truths and
Plenty of falsehoods. But lying is as
Far from truth as the dead from the living.
It was never my intention to do
Either —Just to keep bailing this open
Boat drifting out toward an infinite sea.

Go for
Since when
Say so
Touch blends
Still race
Come cleft
Slides rent
Bolt spent
Scent cusps
Frog spore
Guts quilt
Ace moor

Hovers
mourn us
even before we
die, as
if
life ended
eons ago and
we're just
afterthoughts.
Depths skew
things blowing static
peers into
barely
equivalent edges.
Causality is a
foregone conclusion
about
a lost
fact. Clocks don't
know what
time
it is
any more than
we do.

FOR REAL

Reality don't lie. For real
The truth's what's foundering there.

Truth is found in the morning's light
That every noon puts out of sight.

Liars move on, the lie remains:
Lies that truth enshrines and engrains.

fast
it moves out
like the tide swift flowing
or your love
when you turn away

ERRATA

For "red" read "I should not have done it, should have left it alone,
I don't know what came over me or why I could not, try as I might,
overcome it." For "oceanic" read "leeward, as when the ball dribbles its
way to the center of the earth and the heart barely hears its own beat
but never fails to heed yours." For "lard" read "a studied casualness that
disguises genuine casualness." For "incandescent" read "drowned in
love's apposite fortunes, leering at gushes in the gust of a fragrance."
For "thimbled" read "record-breaking heat reducing statutes to mud
puddles and ideas to pruning hooks." For "cyclic" read "swollen." For
"brush briskly for five minutes with a capon-minder" read "off-limits."
For "crustacean" read "crustacean." For "you be my gracious refuge
now, song" read "why do you rouse my soul and stir up the past?; be
merciful, desist, desist, let the embers of my joy be." For "daemonic dis-
possession" read "season of mist and mellow fruitlessness."

it's harder to
forget than
remember
except when
remembering
what you forgot
and forgetting
what's recalled

LOOSE CANONS

CEIL'S SEAL COAT

I never played catch
with my father but
then he never played
catch with me.

COOL, CALM, AND DRY

If you've got the time, we've got the beer.

THE JEWISH STATE

Hard to get a read.

COOKIE WISE (THE WAY IT CRUMBLES)

& pound foolish.

DIVIDED LOYALTIES

Intersectionality in reverse.

JEW HUNTING ONLY IN SEASON

Permit required.

GOLDEN RULE

Maybe they haven't
blossomed yet or it's
too late.

No re-entry from this poem.

1
idea with green
chooses
event over
redding

2
what's what

3
obtuse hypnotist
truncates
foreforeground

4
sensation dissolves
crooked path
z-sited

5
claw's falls

6
V

7
lush lack

8
slide by slide
(the lace between)

9
Too True

why's (almost) y

10
sold old cold told

11
wh(y) knot

12
you turn

13
Cut Above

could wood
only bite
(where, there)

14
the ladle is a cracked cradle

15
criss almost crossed
unawares
(spackle me again)

16
the subject is still

17
3-D

accordion to whom
accord him his doom

18
just one time

19
AST
UNG
OUTH
ORN
OTION
ONGS
ORTH

20
parent mumbles
have no crumbles
up side this
•
apparent stumbles
have no rumbles
lop ply shifts

21
house mouths
apes gape

22
ouch

(DON'T SLOUCH)

23
who would have thought?

24
edges eating

25
Blue Ridge Mountains

(count them)

for Richard Tuttle

RÜCKENFIGUR

what's true's
glue false
fierce living
loved livid
lured lost
lard

AS I LOVE

As I love:
My poetics
—Zukofsky, "A"-12

A POET SUPREME

I've gOt sPaSmodIc rhYthM yOu've got **il-li-li-lo-(o!)-*q*-shuN** As
seNsOry mode / or release, g(-el-eL-)ation, revER-(b)urr-er-er-
atIon, recoMbinatiOn, oVerlAy, impppUlse, proPulSe, dash-0'-tHe-
puddinGed-puddLe-minded *breath turn* AS woE-inGLy wiGkles,
waitiNg, whOa-wh-w-hImsey, jeRkeD as celeStial harmoniCs/ harm-
onicKs, so sL(0!)W yOu can heAr the vibRatIons lasHing agaInSt
tHe dOrmeRs. <<¶§∞¢£¶>> *ich habe einen spontanen*
Rhythmus, du hast il-li-li-lo- (o!) - q-sun als
sensor-modus / oder freigabe, g (-el-el-) aktion,
ÜberLieB, Atmen drehen sich wie wEi-ingly: dOrMeRen
hören können. ⟨§∿⇒→∞>⇐ʒ↑⇑∿⪵⋔⇐. IncLudiNg but
not limItEd t0. ⇐ʒ∞>↑ dreamT (screamT) beComEs wHiPlaSh /
wishlist w-w-wiTHerEd wHisPs, SprUnG suCcessiOn oVertoWeD to
dArn-daRe-upSter FLOURESCENT **eMManaShUNs**, sHoWereD by
bL0o(uh)ms, beGaLeD, likk*k*e a GahZheal doink bAcK fl00ps on a
corn foLD. //√¶§∞•≠\\ *incluindo, mas não limitado >>*
sonhou (grita) benewlal / w-w-werered, pesquisado
por bloo (uh) bem-vindo, talvez um em um fiorde
de dobra. ⟨§∿⇒→ʒ↑>⇐⇑∿⪵⋔∞⇐. What a FluKe! iF I
cOulD onLy sing 0ut o' temmpi-MENTAL. **CrEaTiOnIsMus(e)** begins
here. mInEd-f0rGed in surrep(E)titious eruptions (scrum-uhm-p-
p-p-tious), mired |) smeared (| in *tenebrae*—aCcouStic tAcTil(t)itY
nigh onto sTeAm pour-r-r-r-ing (purrrrring) oUt of man(w)Hole. →
ʒ↑>⇐⇑⟨⇒§∿∿⪵⋔∞⇐ Qu'est-ce qu'un FluKe! Si
je ne faisais que chanter |]} commence ici dans
éruptions mérieuses, embourbés |) enduit (| dans
le tenebrae - tactilité acoustique [inclinaison]
près de la vapeur qui sort de la bouche d'égout.
INCLUS, mais pas limité à. **caL-Q!-luSt** *of* inter-per-s0nic
quest-IONs. thE makiNg iS the RE:seiveing, roiLinG with *&* againSt—
aLl tH(w)aætttt re-v(h)eAls in rE-veiliNg.

for Cecil Taylor

Patience will get you only so far
And with and what and whether
See it bounce on the razor wire perimeter
I'd gamble the full three and seven
And with and what and whether
Reliance is a thing for warmer weather
See it bounce on the razor wire perimeter
A friend in need fills me with terror
I'd gamble the full three and seven
There's only so much taste in a feather
Patience will get you only so far
Reliance is a thing for warmer weather
Objects in the distance mostly go unseen
There's only so much taste in a feather
If you know please tell me so
The hedgehog in the bush is worth twice the one in dreams
Objects in the distance mostly go unseen
I've a mind to pickle lima beans
A friend in need fills me with terror
The hedgehog in the bush is worth twice the one in dreams
I've a mind to pickle lima beans
If you know please tell me so

It really bugs me when you say that, man.
Like, I mean, it's not my bag, man. You are
bumming me out. Maybe it's the other
guy's bag, maybe it's your bag, man, but it's
not my bag. No how no way. What a drag.
So uncool. I got my own bag, man.
& I don't need that bag. Can you dig that?
I'm telling you, man, you're really chilling
my vibe. My bag is mellow, man, & I
don't dig what's coming down. Like I say, man
it's not my bag.

SONG

I got what I got
take what I take
I like what I like
hate what I hate

THIS POEM IS NOT IN SERVICE

I get pork at the pork store
Money at the bank
Love in the outfield
Then I draw a blank

I've wandered long and far
Never left the block
Come to me at midnight
To shake like skimming rocks

Been on my own
For the first 99 degrees
Never felt bitter
Till I lost the telephone

Johnny-come-lately
With a cane and a screw
Every time hear your name
Dive into a stew

Nowhere to find myself
When I got back
Polka dot hairpiece
Hieroglyphs on a lark

Still waters make me thirsty
They rumple my brain
Save the date for sacrifice
Now it's time for blame

Shell-shocked and counting
Fills my head with quarrels
Museum in the basement
Attic infested with mouths

Give me 50 dollars
I'll buy you a diamond ring
Give me the keys to your heart
I'll lock it up and throw away the recipe

Cause I used to be somebody
Never mind the price of the fall
One day you're on top of the world
Before you know it, no place at all.

You break it
you bought into
it. We were
the fire before
the fire was
ours. Now it's
theirs. There is
no hope greater
than despair &
despair is no
hope at all.

SHANTY

bury me at sea, sea, sea
that's where I want to be, be, be
beyond all care, care, care
near to nowhere, where, where

MARINE

Ardent char of swirl—
Acid prow of ardency—
Battered cum
Salves such renouncing
As currents surge
On ornery immensity of flux
Verge east in circular refulgence—
Verses' pilloried forest
Verses' jettisoned fit—
Where angles hurt light's turbulence.

after Rimbaud

That's a killer ape, just don't
expect me to marinate it. Sure
sure, I get it, if it's not my
problem, pass the stickly
bougainvilleas and keep on
trusting. Only I seem to
miss every even beat in a
road. Might as well say
hazelnut grounds of unperturbed
timeliness. I hit the brakes
too late, story of my inky
reprobation.

I can swim
better than
talk
& walking's
just the same
if I
remember
how.
Swim against
tide,
tire quicker
(I do) . . .
or when
you let
tide
rule &
you're pulled
under.
The echo of
the mountains
on the lake,
just like
for oodles of
years. But
at your back
the lake is
bound by
Metro Anywhere.
It's local v.
universal, to
belabor the
shibboleth.
A few

blocks away
shirts
blowing on
tenement
line,
just like
the home
I thought
I
imagined. No
one will
believe
this of
vast import
to the nation.

Even when it was a virgin
It was not a virgin

But as for now
Let's make a date
In the wake of fate
(You see the stakes
Were make or break).
When history vanishes
We're on our own
Without an oar
Like totally shorn.
When the then then
Is nowhere now
It's an ontological mess
To make up for
All this damn
Unmitigated stress.
No then is likewise
No now now, a finger
Pointing to itself or
Sky without horizon.
Be here then
And be there
When. Moment's
rush's a rainbow.

What did I tell you? And you never
listen, either. Never did, never do.
Half a loaf's not as good as none.
No distraction. And when you get
there you forget what you came for.
Little matter as long as the restlessness
doesn't turn to full-scale psychosis,
or even if it did, who are you to talk?

DISORDERS OF ARTICULATION

Lament's too common,
grief unsteady. Dish
cracked just enough to
almost break. We live on
the line, or love to.

for Peter Gizzi

How difficult, Yiddish, for me;
even father, the Yiddish for, Hebrew, tongue
's foreign. Like home never had
or ones do.

for Ariel Resnikoff

YOUR CAR IS THAR
The tempo, see
Demagnetizer
Like a sandwich
Near a rodeo
Some cucumber
Interdicts

AUTORETORTROBOT
In an espied olio
reflexion's agile dad
borrows nutritious movement
LA's lines disabuse tantrums
viscous corridors—last imagined
dejected hacks—inacceptable, pearls
simply in the conversation—tan, utter
conned monstrous miasmas. Simply
provokes choice, churls, an uncle in circa
forms chrysalis, affiliations of the duh, da.

NONCE, LO, SUFFICIENT MINT
Nonce, lo, sufficient mint
levitates last fall's doze, nuts
those pantaloons, facile mints
elopes with Del's lugars Mel's success
vertigo announces in the shaker
or horizontal indefinite mint
why one in cage in Del's
mar last enigmas

HEY, QUEEN, ME A PUN APORIA

Hey, Queen, me a pun aporia
pour desire aside a phrase
singed makes—combs a freeze
pour no to mar lag or beads as
preoccupations, for a phrase
conned and pummeled—combs a freeze

after Esteban Pujals Gesalí

THE THRESHOLD

waking to
bathroom noise
thinking she's
sleeping beside
him takes
gun under
pillow lunges
toward clamor
shoots through
door. scream.
blood pours
over threshold.

re: Oscar Pistorius

THEORY OF POTTERY

You brought it
you bake it. Never forgive a succor on a
break. To
receive is to be easily burned. Once
smitten, argue for
slide. Invictus today
toady anon. There's less to
appearance than it seems. Elude
elision and the
swamp will suck the bejesus even from a
rock. Better to overpay than
buy a lemon. Better to buy
a lemon than get
squeezed. Better squeezed than
hung out
to dry. Better hung out to dry than be
buried alive. Fancy is
at the root of illusion and the soul
of truth.—A kick in the ass will never
abolish asses.

Jews are
scapegoated
& this makes us
hypervigilant
against scapegoating
Jews but this
hypervigilance
compromises our
judgment so we
scapegoat Jews
to avoid
bias

THE WAGES OF PASCAL

My mind's abind in double and thriple blinds
Scarcely can I see what's right in front of me
I stumble and stare at things no longer there
My head's in the hopper, unscrambled by doppler
The planet is warming but not to me
I did it and do it and take no responsibility
Art's a drag, thinking a bore
I pretend to doodle but to tell the truth I'm sore
No doubt these rhymes annoy you
But, face it, it's because they suit you to a tee
What happened to disjunction, parasols, and ennui?

a
line is
a
terrible thing
to waste.

*

you
break it
you
thought it.

*

don't break
it—
spend it.

DOUBLE BLIND

there are secrets I know
but never told
because they're still
secret to me

If you can't stand the sand, get off the beach.
If you can't bear the bother, seek nirvana.
If you can't take Daytona, it's not the heat
It's the Republicans.

THE AUNT OF MY UNCLE IS
THE COUSIN OF MY NEPHEW

Restive foreshadowing delays
Mourners' piercing pulse
Even as is likely slotted for
Done heartening deplore
Quick messenger in place
Along soldier bars or calming
Grave, the more the more
Intends when scrape embroiders
Fleece-like airs where terraced
Front aborts their frame.

SOMEWHERE BETWEEN HOPELESSNESS
AND DESPAIR IS A STOP CALLED POETRY

Get out now.

SELF-STRIKE DAY

We have suffered under the oppressive weight of ourselves far too long.

- refuse to listen to yourself
- break all financial ties to yourself
- refuse to acknowledge family members and friends
- boycott job
- sign off social media
- relinquish authority
- actively protest your consciousness

remember: I *is the problem.*

Sappho is too cerebral
Laozi cannot be categorized
Buddha is the real thing
Confucius does not communicate
Homer is a witch
Heraclitus no longer has affect
Aeschylus is easy
Sophocles communicates
Euripides is too emotional
Socrates is a fake
Aristophanes is too emotional
Isocrates is a fake
Plato is not emotional enough
Diogenes is morally repugnant
Aristotle cannot be categorized
Longinus is abstract
Epicurus is not emotional
Cicero is rhetorical
Julius Caesar is elitist
Lucretius is not emotional enough
Catullus is hypocritical
Virgil is a sycophant
Ovid is solipsistic
Jesus is the real thing
St. Augustine is morally repugnant
Maimonides is difficult
Thomas Aquinas is difficult
Guido Cavalcanti is elitist
Cimabue is heartless
Dante loves God
Giotto cannot be categorized
Petrarch is a conformist
Chaucer is misunderstood

Brunelleschi brought me to tears
Van Eyck lacks heart
Fra Angelico is too emotional
Leon Battista Alberti is spiritual
Piero Della Francesca is psychedelic
Crivelli is dogmatic
Memling is artless
Botticelli is enmeshed in fantasy
Lorenzo de Medici is hypocritical
Bosch is awkward
Mantegna is perfect
Leonardo da Vinci is too emotional
Savonarola is too cerebral
Skelton is dogmatic
Machiavelli is affirmative
Erasmus is not emotional enough
Michelangelo is morally repugnant
Titian is a barrel of laughs
Giorgione is sincere
Thomas More is heartless
Montezuma is a witch
Raphael swings
Luther leaves me wanting more
Cortés is affirmative
Rabelais is cynical
Correggio is trendy
Holbein is not emotional enough
Bronzino is abstract
Wyatt is not affirmative
Surrey is free of dogma
Parmigiano does not conform
Montaigne is contradictory
St. John of the Cross suffers fools gladly
Cervantes is a fake
Spencer has affect
Sidney is accessible

Annibale Carracci is narcissistic
Bacon is riddled with riddles
Dowland is a real human being
Marlowe is heartless
Shakespeare is delusional
Galileo has a Jewish cast of mind
Caravaggio is not emotional enough
Monteverdi is humble
Campion is too ideological
Donne makes sense
Ben Johnson is too cerebral
Guido Reni is a nihilist
Rubens is compliant
Herrick is incomprehensible
George Herbert is perfectly clear
Descartes is too cerebral
Poussin has affect
Van Dyck shows courage
Cromwell is enmeshed in fantasy
Velázquez is a conformist
Rembrandt is defiant
Milton is too ideological
Bradstreet is sincere
Corneille is not affirmative
Andrew Marvell is a formalist
La Fontaine is universal
Blaise Pascal is not spiritual enough
Dryden is free of ideology
Spinoza is too cerebral
Locke is humorless
Vermeer is hallucinatory
Racine is ironic
Newton is anthropocentric
Edward Taylor is idealistic
Leibniz is queasy
Cotton Mather is misanthropic

Swift is too cerebral
Vico is emotionless
Watteau is racist
Handel is a fake
Bach is perfect
Scarlatti is dated
Bishop Berkeley is the real thing
Pope is fairly androgynous
Richardson is clumsy
Jonathan Edwards is a fake
Fielding is too spiritual
Samuel Johnson is ideological
David Hume is a fairy
Diderot is not emotional enough
Laurence Sterne is clownish
Thomas Gray is a drunk
William Collins is precarious
Rousseau is free of ideology
Smollett expresses a female point of view
Kant leaves me cold
Moses Mendelssohn has a Jewish cast of mind
Oliver Goldsmith is professional
Cowper is a coward
Fragonard is inconsistent
James Macpherson is arrogant
Tom Paine is ethically challenged
Goya is narcissistic
Jacques-Louis David is disappointing
Goethe misses the point
Crabbe is hyperbolic
Burns is adolescent
Danton loves God
Blake is a careerist
Napoleon is a hooligan
Wordsworth is affirmative
Hegel is shallow

Hölderlin is tendentious
Walter Scott is misunderstood
Coleridge is mired in fantasy
Jane Austen is cynical
Schopenhauer is cynical
Byron is uncompelling
Shelley is an intellectual thug
Turner is a nonconformist
John Clare is elitist
Keats is seductive
Thomas Carlyle is deep
Thomas Hood is emotional
Emerson is almost perfect
Hawthorne is hopeless
Mill is soporific
Elizabeth Barrett Browning is pessimistic
Longfellow plays it safe
Whittier does not suffer fools
Felix Mendelssohn is intense
Darwin is transcendent
Tennyson is sentimental
Poe is a formalist
Dickens is not affirmative
Browning is nonsensical
Edward Lear is silly
Büchner is absurd
Kierkegaard is abstract
Trollope is too analytic
Thoreau is sardonic
Marx is adorable
Emily Brontë no longer has affect
Melville swings
Whitman is gibberish
Ruskin is too cerebral
Baudelaire is a dandy
Dostoevsky is a monster

Matthew Arnold is riveting
Dante Rossetti is too decorative
Tolstoy is affirmative
Dickinson is confused
Christina Rossetti is a fake
Lewis Carroll brought me to tears
William Morris loves God
Twain is defiant
Swinburne is joyless
Thomas Hardy is not spiritual
William James is cliquish
Mallarmé is a fake
Henry James takes risks
Hopkins does not have a Jewish cast of mind
Nietzsche is degenerate
Lautrémont is a witch
Van Gogh is solipsistic
Rimbaud is frivolous
Wilde has affect
Freud is sarcastic
Conrad is incorrigible
Housman is exemplary
Yeats is ambiguous
Dowson is morally repugnant

as quick as you run as
quick as they'll catch you
upland on spoons or back-
hand on canastas.

I haven't slept in many
a year—and the fissures
reply, are you measuring
fears?

LOOSE LIPS LIFT ALL SLIPS

It wasn't so long ago
and then it was. Sliding
till you hit false bottom,
wrestling metaphor for
sleep. It wasn't so long
and then it was. I'd
keep saying it but
I know you heard me,
even when you didn't.

I'm not me
nor you you
neither we we
but all's found
in them's they

BUSTER KEATON'S SLEEVE

Verse is a tease
Prose'll please
Poetry's liquor
But prose is quicker

dubious

mild

tornado

dovecoats

imperious

redemption

rustle

myopic

malleable

torso

gizmo

ember

unearthly

truant

Over the top's
not over the hill:
if the boogeyman
don't get you
undertaker will.
It's a day to
tomorrow, feels like
yesterday—everything
keeps speeding up
but today it's way
slow down.
The ins are on the
outs (take it from
me) lima beans
with butter—see
what I mean? One guy
plays a horn, girl
gives a couple of
shouts: inside the morning
papers reality keeps on
lashing out. Feel free to
play victim, feel free to play
cop: never twains meeting
until it's pitch as dark.
It's a day
to tomorrow
feels like
yesterday
everything keeps
speeding up
but today it's so
slow down.

WERE YOU THERE WHEN THEY
CRUCIFIED OUR LORD?

I was. Let me tell you about it. It was mean ugly,
disgusting. Shattering if you really want to know.
And the worst thing is it didn't stop, went on for days,
for years if truth be told. It never stopped.

A UNIFIED THEORY OF POETRY

I don't think so.

TED GREENWALD: *What does it feel like to be a poet in the "postmodern" era?*

[*laughs*] What does it feel like to be anybody in the postmodern era? Is one anybody in the postmodern era? As far as poetry goes, for most people modernism never arrived, so postmodernism seems premature.

Does language have a future?

Language only has a future. And we can find it only in the present. It's too bad many people find the present in language something that makes no sense to them, because if we can't make sense of/with the present then prospects for the future are none too good. And our ability to understand and respond to the past is numbed, if not obliterated.

What about the future of words?

What *about* the future of words! In a sense there are no words, only languages. And languages have no meaning outside their use. So the future of words and languages is dependent on our doing something with them rather than their doing something with us. We are given the words that we use, but we don't have to pronounce them the way we've been taught, or order them as we have been ordered.

Can poetry develop an economy?

Poetry is always involved with economy at many different levels. The question really is, can poetry evade economy, as Romantic ideology seems to suggest. At one level there's the semantic economy of poetry: accumulation and loss, absorption and repellence, excess and limitation. At another level there's the economy of distribution and dissemination: production, context of publication, readings, distribution, response. This second level of poetic economy contributes to the meanings of a poem as much as the first.

What does love got to do with it?

They don't know what love is. I know what love is.

You do?

Love is *only* doing. And acts of love are not the same as talking about them.

What's your sense of the direction poetry's taking as we move into the twenty-first century?

I think that there's a greater understanding that poetry even within a single language like English cannot be understood as a unitary practice. The differences among poetries are incommensurable. And this radical decentralization of expression opens up the potential for communication of a different sort than we've grown accustomed to. You might call this a revolution in democracy. At the same time, one can expect enormous resistance to these developments.

Are you suggesting that art is democratic?

The kind of democracy I'm talking about is not the majority dictating to and restricting the licenses of the minority, but rather a democracy in which the rights of minorities and the particular individuation of their perspectives are not only protected but fostered. The "English First" movement is perhaps the most visible symbol of opposition to the sort of radical democracy I am talking about.

Sort of like endangered species?

Our species *is* endangered. Not only by physical annihilation but also mental annihilation, which means greater and greater uniformity of thought, expression, and conduct. And uniformity is engendered, not limited, by the sorts of "either-or" choices which are a product of our consumer society.

What's your favorite movie of the 80s?

Everybody's already answered that question.

Does poetry require inspiration to be produced?

Yes.

How important is boredom to "modernism"?

I think that boredom is often a way of pointing to the inexplicable and the unknown as much as the mundane. The value of putting forward boredom as a positive feature of a work seems strained at this point, but readers will often find it difficult to involve themselves in that which is totally enthralling. If paradise were put on the market there wouldn't necessarily be that many buyers.

What's your favorite weather?

I don't have a favorite weather. And for that reason I don't like it to stay the same too long. This is also an answer to your last question.

Who gets the horse?

Not the horse trader. And not the rider. Maybe nobody should get the horse. Maybe the horse can just go home.

Who does the dishes?

We alternate.

Who gets the girl?

Not the girl trader. And not the rider. Maybe she can go home too. Maybe.

But you can't go home again?

You could if you found the address.

Any advice to young poets?

Look for the address.

GUSH

Mercury's in retrograde
But I'm over the moon
My life it stood a warped croon
Lost somewhere between Venus
And the Hardscrapple Saloon.
Put my time in abandoned mines
Sailed to Saturn and the Argentine
Uranus's in masquerade
Mars is on the run
August's not yet over
Let's open a bottle of rum.

because they
see my scraggly
beard, my crooked
hat, and the dark
shine from my
glasses, they say
I am a poet

after Léon de Greiff
(Medellín subway)

ECHOLOGS

Damoetas
To all's high, guys! everything that echoes!,
what gives ground and by Jove'll cure our songs.

Menalcas
But it's me that beauty loves!; all her charms
surround, crowns of sweetest ruddy roses.

Damoetas
My girl's cupid, first she creams me with an apple
then slides behind the willows: peek-a-boo.

Menalcas
My guy's no tease: he comes on to me so often
our dogs know him much better than my bitch.

Damoetas
To the gift who is my Venus I give
my place in the sky, where mourning doves fly.

Menalcas
Nine ripe rimes I give the boy today,
a score more love songs are on their way.

Damoetas
The words my lover whispers to me!
Send them on wings for eternity!

Menalcas
Love the love, love, but hate
if you go fishing and leave me nets.

Damoetas
Hey, friend, send me your girl for my birthday,
then come yourself for the after party.

Menalcas
I love that girl best; she was all tears when I left,
O beauty, goodbye, goodbye, said she to her guy.

Damoetas
Grieves. Wolf to sheep, bloom in the storm,
house on fire, our lover's ire.

Menalcas
Sweetens. Flower to bee, liquor from vine,
the rhythms in this song, my lover mine.

Damoetas
Pollio loves our all too rustic runes:
this one's for our patron and his muses.

Menalcas
Pollio's own new poems are ferocious:
no bull just charging aesthetic focus.

Damoetas
Those who love you, Pollio, may they come to you,
like boats come to the shore, as honey for your sores.

Menalcas
Those abide prize crap adore boring poems,
watch them milk jackasses and water stones.

Damoetas
Gather your berries as you may; but guys, better get wise!:
beware that chill snake in the grass who's always in disguise.

Menalcas
A slippery slope, dear lamb, makes treacherous place to stand:
watch those mules ahead, climbing from water onto dry land.

Damoetas
Tommy, keep those kids out of the waves's wrath!,
when the time comes, I'll give them both a bath.

Menalcas
Collect thoughts, boys: if day's heat
nips 'em in bud, our pens will dry.

Damoetas
Hey, hey, can't you see, the bull's going bust!
There's plenty of love but not enough trust.

Menalcas
The tender lambs in our care are skin and bones of despair.
If love you do deny, then all's left is an evil eye.

Damoetas
You will be my god!, but only if you tell me—
where, on earth, sky's no bigger than a purse?

Menalcas
You can take my wife!, but only if you tell me—
where, on earth, petals are inscribed with verse?

With Richard Tuttle
After the poetry match in Virgil's Eclogues, *III*

CALLBACK

I am a motorized car headed for a pockmarked tunnel. Three polar
bears approach, waving, as I lunge for cover in nearby twilight. Green
and yellowed flags flail overhead, swaying like Tommy Dorsey stand-
ins. The trick is to arrive exactly eight minutes late and stay just for the
anthems so there won't be enough time to dance with the heavily armed
producers. The time comes and I'm sweating it out in unremitting tears.
It must be a hundred if it's a day. The first shot of gin burns the throat.
I can't hear what the girl in the ad is saying so I turn to the articles. The
coleslaw is homemade. I fall all over myself but seem serene. I look
down. The luggage tags are smudged with fudge from your hands. Is
that egg on his face—I can still remember the look in your eyes—or
have we secretly left Brooklyn? Nobody remembered to tell me.

I'm not myself.
Then who?
Sick.
And that's not you?
Not the person I otherwise am.
Who's that?
A shadow, a mist, a sorrow.
Wise up and be other.
Self out of self.
Incontinent.

TOMORROW

bring white socks

It is what it was.
It's not what it's not.
It hurts where it hurt.
It cut where it cuts.
It counts when it could.
It strays where it stayed.
It stayed when it strays.
It shudders as it shut.
It dropped as it drops.
It drips as it dripped.
It was what it is.

A's on the F
& D's
the C,
but only
in sector B,
then
runs on N
till becoming
A again.
R's local
on express,
otherwise it's
think Q & G.
L skips
all stops while
O
terminates
unexpectedly:
take
shuffle bus
if available
or transfer
to V
when possible

.

No
weekend service
on M, T, & E
until June 22, 2023.
Signal problems
on X: expect
delays on the Y & Z.
Late night

service
suspended on every
other line
for an indeterminate
time.

The life lives after the life
As a seed is a void in the world-as-is
Opening paths to worlds-could-be.
If and as, where and when, remains
Sewn into the Heavenly Garment
Of the Unknown, halfway between there
And hereafter, lodged in an either
Of times' remorseless ether
(Concoctions and fever).
Justice is never abstract but we
Abstract it at mineral peril, against
Bodies laid waste in the pillage—
Hope's desperate pilgrimage.

A poem is not a monument, but my nomination for an American hero worthy of commendation is Shields Green. Green, who had liberated himself from slavery, was twenty-three in 1859 when he was executed by the Commonwealth of Virginia as a result of his participation in the armed struggle against slavery led by John Brown. Green had met Brown at the home of Frederick Douglass. While Douglass declined to join Brown, he reports that Green said, "'I b'leve I'll go wid de ole man.' . . . Shields Green was not one to shrink from hardships or dangers. He was a man of few words, and his speech was singularly broken; but his courage and self-respect made him quite a dignified character." Douglass also reported that rather than escape capture after Harpers Ferry, "he simply said he must go down to de ole man." In an article on Green's trial, Steven Lubet notes that Green's lawyer successfully argued that *Dred Scott* (decided just two years earlier) established that Green could not be charged with treason since he was not an enfranchised citizen who owed allegiance to the state. Denied the vote, Green had no obligation to be loyal to Virginia or to the US. With the treason charge thrown out, Green was convicted of murder and conspiracy. After the hanging, Green's body was seized for defilement by dissection by medical students from Winchester, Virginia. Lubet reports that six years later the town of Oberlin created a memorial to Green and two other Brown freedom fighters from Oberlin. "These colored citizens of Oberlin," the inscription reads, "the heroic associates of the immortal John Brown, gave their lives for the slave. *Et nunc servitudo etiam mortua est, laus deo.*"

Frederick Douglass, *The Life and Times of Frederick Douglass* (Hartford, CT: Park, 1882), 187–92.

Steven Lubet, "Execution in Virginia, 1859: The Trials of Green and Copeland." Faculty Working Papers 209. Evanston, IL: Northwestern University, 2012, 11–12, 25–26. scholarlycommons.law.northwestern.edu/facultyworkingpapers/209.

This page is closed for deinstallation.

aS if sTumbLing iNto pItChEd nIgHt
inFusEd wiTh the muSiC of neW ligHt

oNe nOte aT a

tiMe, torQu-

(E)

ing off tH-

e neX-

t

consTelLatI

ons of uNe-

vEn

sou-

Nd in

pRec-

ise cH-

oRdal

re-artIc-

ulA-

tIons. aS on

                              tHe mOon thE
        foOd is nEveR the sAme aS

                                              at

                                                       h-

        oMe untiL tHerE iS

                          [no home or it's]

                tHe

                      onLy hoM-

e yoU k-

                now. I meAn

                      t-

        he senSe of belOng

                                    iNg. Hod-

                gEs moRe than striKes tHe
                      ri-
        ght noTes, he uSh-

                      eRs yoU inTo thE seN-

                sU-

                          oUs

                                    immmmmmm-

ediaCy of the iMp-

robabLe.

for Brian Ferneyhough and Nicolas Hodges

ARS IMPOTENS

Poetry is made not of ideas but of words.
Poetry is not made of ideas but words.
Poetry's made not of ideas but of words.
Of words, poetry's made, not ideas.
Words is what poetry is made of, not ideas.
Not of ideas, poetry's made of words.
Is made of words, poetry, not ideas.
Made not of ideas but words, poetry.

exhaustion follows hard labor
also profligacy

strong wind breaks even the mightiest bough
and lots of us twigs on the way

even the most difficult path
is a beginning

every lie's a kind of truth

truth is never sincere

the greatest care is a form
of ontological abandon

hope wounds eternity

feelings are heartless

trust is cozened by cruelty

before every step
is a step

the hardest step is
before the first

first step is standing still

what the kind lack in intelligence
the intelligent lack in kindness

North of the north pole
South of desire
I found my love
Lone and grey
Sailing for the morrow.
"How far is that?"
I asked, despaired
But she'd not tell
Not even to wind's
whispering spells.
Though flash of
Cosmos was in our
Sights, we'd little hope
Prolong the night.
Little hope but lots
Of whines, living already
On leveraged time.
Little hope and plenty
Of rime, here in a
Muddled middle
Piping signs.

And boy is it scary.

LIKE KNIGHTS PASSING OUT ON A SHIP

The nuns are
running quicklier than
the cork gets
goosed (livers set
aside for later).
I nixed the
last glance in
the third tier
of the Vagabonding.
(Overlooked the blinds.)
The toys are
praying hard on
the deck oblivious
to reproaching gales.
—"Dad, you want
to play kike
with me?"—"How
many times have
I told you, we
should have bought
better ailerons?" Time's
fixed, it's us
keeps drifting, having
severed the tether
to the mother
lode. This is
the poem you
always say no
one writes—about
that first landing
on the moon.

for Christian Bök

Poetry is best that governs least.

No it isn't.

Poetry and citizenship are inconsolably incommensurable, conjoined at the heart but beating time to different drummers.

From time to time.

Aesthetic justice is symbolic and dwells next to, not in, the world of political action.

Give me a break!

The politics of poetic form is averse to the form of political prose.

In your dreams!

The kind of poetry I want is precarious and extreme, the kind of citizenship I want is neither.

As if you can have it both ways.

Accessibility is to prose what opacity is to poetry.

As in: a long walk is better than a short peer?

The dollar value of poetry can be calculated as the square root of the sublime times the negative sum of utopia divided by the excess derivative of anoriginality.

You wish!

The kind of poetry I want questions norms of identity by rocking and roiling. It traffics in error and errancy. It's a querulous query. But that's not the only kind of poetry I want.

You could fool me, buddy.

When language grapples with the unfamiliar or repressed, it will more likely sound strange than familiar.

The strange is pretty familiar to me.

Politics speaks truth to power. Poetry speaks truth to truth.

Poetry is necessarily plural; its strands are inimical to one another.

Poetry is just as vital when it is refused by public space as when it occupies public space. The question is not why discomforting poetry (to use a phrase of Tonya Foster's) doesn't have a public voice in America today, but why that voice is cast aside.

The question is not "Is Poetry Dead?" (again) but "Why are you dead to poetry?"

Poetry is not an export product of suffering or beauty, solidarity or despair, but a domain of freedom shrouded in veils, an unextractable aesthetic ore.

Poetry is a form of lamentation, not, to split cares, an expression of lamentation.

Aesthetic justice turns an otherworldly eye to family, nation, community, and rationality. Poetry so conceived is of the earth, not of the world. This is how poetry matters in the world.

Aesthetic privilege is a negative market force, an active agent of loss.

Poetry emerges from difficult life *in spite of* as much as *a result of.*

So much depends upon spite.

The promise of a poem, the kind of poetry I want, is that it refuses reality.

But is it good for the Jews?

To be a poetic citizen is not to act as a citizen but to perform as a poet. But there can be no citizenship without poetry. Even citizenship is symbolic. Citizenship that refuses dialogue with the delirious, wanton, discomforting possibilities of poetry approaches nativism.

Get off your low horse.

If citizenship is the first language of the democrat, then poetry is a second language that, out of love and deep need, refuses to obey its mother tongue.

Poetry has no purpose and that is not its purpose.

nothing like
luck
'cept
none,
nothing
like
song
save
songs.
Trees
freeze
breeze,
so
we, staring
at
stars with
stormy
tears,
eyes
undressing
night's
caressing.

for Enrique Winter

Sometimes, not that I can say when
Rain becomes mist, I mean even
When it's pouring. I get wet
But feel close to earth, which
After all, I've only seen on TV.
There is a scattering that pretends
To oblige, but there's no freedom
In that either.

H MARKS THE SPOT

1. Hermes arrives from remote location, looking haggard, carrying hymnal and hatchet.
2. Helen of Troy picks a fight with hermaphrodite with halo.
3. Heraklitus goes skinny dipping in Housatonic.
4. A high school honor guard, separated from troupe, wanders into a harem.
5. Haunted hippies re-create scene from Beatles' *Help!*
6. H.D. in hallway with huge hook.
7. The hem is like the hem, the head is like the head, the hole is like the . . .
8. Homosexual hosiery hoisted.
9. Herodotus reads headlines.
10. Hip hopelessness.
11. A local hero marches down a hall filled with Hindu statues.
12. Hanoi is bombed.
13. Billie Holiday hums hexameters.
14. An ad for Preparation H.
15. Hunger is stronger than happiness.
16. Holy is the hoot of the hyena.
17. "Sieg Heil! Sieg Heil! Right in der fuehrer's face!"
18. Hamlet having a ham sandwich at the Horn & Hardart automat.
19. Hitler in high heels.
20. How to hit a homer.
21. Hitchcock's hair.
22. Heading home.
23. Hurt lurks in hitherto hallowed halls.
24. Host's hocked helmet.
25. Jello again.
26. Holograph of hat.
27. Hooray for Hollywood.
28. Helsinki hack bound for Honolulu.
29. "Heaven, I'm in heaven . . ."
30. Hölderlin hollering in tower.

31. Hell is the eternal loss of one you love.
32. "Hold it, I think you're gonna like this picture." (Bob Cummings)
33. Heinrich Heine posing with Lorelei.
34. Homer in a coffee shop having a hamburger.
35. Hercules, hotel doorman.
36. History unfolds in a crawl on Times Square news ticker.
37. There's no hell like my hell. My hell is the best hell there is.
38. Handle on the door of my house.
39. Hiccups erupt.
40. Hysteric breaks into hysterics.
41. Hysteric is put in harness.
42. Hallucination: none of this is illusion; even the hallucination is not a hallucination.
43. Harpo plays harpsichord.
44. Harmonizing heterogeneity.
45. A hundred heroin highs, a hundred herons fly.
46. Houdini escapes.
47. Hypnotist puts me under a spell from which I never awake.
48. Some hurts never heal.
49. Hospital corners on hospital bed.
50. Heave ho, heave ho.

Scenario for Henry Hills's film centering on the letter H
& in memory of Warren Sonbert

ANYHOW

a
  poem
  doesn't
  change
  the
  world
  doesn't
  change
  minds
  doesn't
    change
  hearts
  that
  is
  the
  beauty
  of
    poetry
  and
  why
  politics
    without
  poetics
    will
  always
  end
    up
  with
  one
    more
  round
  of
    same

What you heard is not what I said.
COMMENTARY: You are lying.
COMMENTARY: "What is said" is never absolute.
COMMENTARY: *Meaning is always contextual.*

As the crow flies, so flies the Jew.
COMMENTARY: The Jew exists both in everyday life and in the imaginary.
COMMENTARY: Diaspora is never a whole story.
COMMENTARY: *Low overhead is ideal.*

"Lies are truths that have hardened" (Alan Davies).
COMMENTARY: On the contrary—Truth is lies that have hardened.
COMMENTARY: The problem is not lies but liars.
COMMENTARY: *Truth is difficult.*

"We are rats who build the labyrinth from which we plan to escape"
(Raymond Queneau on OuLiPo practice).
COMMENTARY: On the contrary—We are rats who build labyrinths
from which we cannot escape.
COMMENTARY: On the contrary—We are labyrinths who build man.
(Even labyrinths have fathers.)
COMMENTARY: *Animalady is a condition, not a worldview.*

Stop putting mouths in my words.
COMMENTARY: Resistance precedes presence.
COMMENTARY: Poetry is not speech but speech sounds.
COMMENTARY: *Words are not just what is spoken.*

"Phatic not vatic" (Runa Bandyopadhyay).
COMMENTARY: Echopoetics.
COMMENTARY: Identities not identity.
COMMENTARY: [Intentionally left blank]

Knowing what I know today, that much less than before.
COMMENTARY: How much beyond all is whatever is and is today.
COMMENTARY: Even as now is not now and then was not then, still time moves forward, but once and again stops for passengers.
COMMENTARY: *To know nothing is the only positive form of knowledge.*

Metonymy is destiny.
COMMENTARY: Did I tell you to sing?
COMMENTARY: The sun is greater than its sparks.
COMMENTARY: *Even the echoes have echoes.*

The enemy of my enmity is my calamity.
COMMENTARY: Don't say "I told you so" until you're wrong.
COMMENTARY: Indignation intensifies heartburn but is preferable to heart failure.
COMMENTARY: *The enemy of my enmity is my sentimentality.*

The only thing harder than being a poet is being married to one.
COMMENTARY: A reworking of Reb Gimlet's "The only thing harder than being a fool is being married to one," itself a reworking of Reb Negroni's "The only thing harder than being a Jew is being married to one," itself a reworking of Reb Gibson's "The only thing harder than being God is being married to God."
COMMENTARY: Married in the sense of any long-standing intimate relationship.
COMMENTARY: *"Poet" here signifies verbal hurdles/hurtles to enlightenment.*

Quantum mechanics commands our respect. But an inner voice tells me that this is not yet the real McCoy. The theory provides a lot, but it hardly brings us nearer the old mystery. Anyway, I'm convinced that it's not a throw of the dice ["Die Quantenmechanik ist sehr achtunggebietend. Aber eine innere Stimme sagt mir, daß das doch nicht der wahre Jakob ist. Die Theorie liefert viel, aber dem Geheimnis des Alten bringt sie uns kaum näher. Jedenfalls bin ich überzeugt, daß der nicht würfelt"] (Albert Einstein).

COMMENTARY: But it could be pinochle.
COMMENTARY: Science will never abolish poetry.
COMMENTARY: *"Nah ist / Und schwer zu fassen der Gott"* (Hölderlin).

Wish, desire, need denied; love hides.
COMMENTARY: An arrow to the heart kills you as dead as a stab in the back.
COMMENTARY: Inside the folds of language are the folds of things.
COMMENTARY: *The hidden pierces the visible at the circumference of the conscious.*

I cannot forgive what I blame you for but which you haven't done.
COMMENTARY: Worse than anything we do is what we fail to do, not by effort but by inattention.
COMMENTARY: Consciousness is culpability.
COMMENTARY: *Irresponsibility is the inability to respond.*

Forget Being, it never liked you anyway.
COMMENTARY: The sign on the screen says, "Access Denied."
COMMENTARY: For Marjorie Perloff: Being is a club that beats you to the ground at closing time, then opens the next day as if nothing had happened.
COMMENTARY: For Felix Bernstein: *Being stumbles, time evaporates, only the traces of trances persist.* (Dasein stolpert, zeit ist verflogen, nur die Spuren der Trance bleiben bestehen.)

For love has such a spirit that if it is portrayed it dies ["Ch'Amor mi dona—un spirito in suo stato / che, figurato,—more"] (Cavalcanti).
COMMENTARY: That Love gives me—a spirit in such state / that, figured,—dies.
COMMENTARY: "From Love is won a spirit, in some wise, / Which dies perpetually" (Rossetti).
COMMENTARY: *"For Love me gives a spirit on his part / Who dieth if portrayed"* (Pound).

Great wisdom's clumsy, true eloquence stutters. [大巧若拙, 大辯若訥] (*Tao Te Ching* 45).

COMMENTARY: For Feng Yi: Wisdom is awkward and unruly, eloquence stammers and stumbles.

COMMENTARY: For Ariel Resnikoff: There is nothing more bent than the straight.

COMMENTARY: After Adorno: *The appearance of authenticity is a fabrication.*

Translation is the mother of invention and the father of misunderstanding.

COMMENTARY: Better to stand under, nearer, than to touch. Better still: in between. (Besser unter, näher, als zum Anfassen. Besser noch: Zwischendurch.)

COMMENTARY: "You know the story of Russian history, centuries of mayhem and suffering. . . . Then the bad times begin" (Philip Nikolayev).

COMMENTARY: *The authenticity of fabrication is appearance.* (Die Authentizität der Herstellung ist das Aussehen.)

Translation has both an asymptotic desire for closeness verging on fusion and an opposite impulse to distance, to retreat from the otherness of its utterance. These impulses are antipodal and irreconcilable yet reciprocal and, for Hölderlin, ultimately and precariously the same (nach Sieburth).

COMMENTARY: "Let no one / Reproach the beauty / Of my homegrown speech / As I go to the fields / Alone, where the lily / Grows wild, without fear" (Sieburth). "Und nicht soll einer / Der Rede Schonheit mir / Die heimadiche, vorwerfen, / Dieweil ich allein / Zum Felde gehe, wo wild / Die Lilie wachst, furchdos" (Hölderlin).

COMMENTARY: "But we shall not look forward / Or back. Let ourselves rock, as / On a boat, lapped by waves" (Sieburth). "Vorwarts aber und riikwarts wollen wir / Nicht sehn. Uns wiegen lassen, wie / Auf schwankem Kahne der See" (Hölderlin).

COMMENTARY: *"Veiled in song"* (Sieburth). *"Ins Lied / Gehüllt"* (Hölderlin).

For Richard Sieburth at 70

ANTI-METAPHYSICAL POEM

There's no fantasy like reality
(Though reality's not fancy at all)
No thing so real as truth
(Yet the truth's not real at all)
No, nothing so true as reality's call
Truth enmeshed in layers of thrall
(Fantasies of imagination and nothing more)

Abolens sensus numquam liberare cogitatione.
Abolishing reason will never free thought.

•

Etiam homo fastus scribere posse bonum carmen. Sed suus non amo.
Even a self-righteous man can write a good poem. But it's not likely.

•

Praecaveo osor qui clamat "odisti!"
Beware the bigot who shouts out "bigot!"

•

Nonnumquam homo qui mendacii loquimini veritatem.
Even a liar sometimes must tell the truth.

•

O dii magna! Protecut nobis adversum malis qui consumuntur per justitia.
May the gods save us from those consumed by their righteousness.

•

Colaphus est chiridotus punctum.
A cuff is not a sleeve.
(*Alt.*: A blow is not the full chemise.)

•

Aestas alga mutates in hiberna malogranatum.
Summer seaweed becomes winter pomegranates.

•

Si paratextus fortior poema sequitur fornicando fortior amor?
If paratext is more important than poem, does it follow that love is more important than sex?

•

Perceptio est scriptum.
Perception is textual.

•

Omni scriptura est pupilla.
All texts are orphans.

-

Perspicientia est sensus vigalantis.
Knowledge is a matter of minding sense.

-

Ubi erraverit caper detondetur vitulum.
Where the goat strays the calf is shorn.

-

Rarus est maeror nomas.
Seldom is grief misplaced.

-

Omne iter fluxum.
Every journey takes a turn.

-

Cultura est opinabilis.
Cultivation is a manner of opinion.

-

In fragmenta veritas.
Truth is in pieces.

-

Vivis et vigeo. Argumentum injustitia deos.
The fact that you are alive and thriving is proof that the gods are
not just.

-

Remissio prope nihil. Desiderium dono divum.
Forgiveness is overrated. Regret is a gift of gods.

-

Quid nunc videtur priori numquam imaginabilis.
What was unimaginable an hour ago is unforgettable now.
(unimaginable / hours ago / unforgettable / now)

-

Proximi sui ruina unius hominis felicitatem.
One man's catastrophe is his neighbor's good fortune.

-

Servus absolvo illusion licentia. Dominus amat fraudis.
A slave is free of the illusion of freedom from which his master takes
pleasure.

- Virtus est selectivam.
Virtue is selective.

- Coitus est bonitas plus quam amor. Est tangibili.
Sex is more virtuous than love because it is more tangible.

- Amor abducit lubido.
Love turns many from desire.

- In vino exiguum clinamen veritas.
In wine truth swerves.

- Sensus mentis dolum.
Perception is the finest trick of the mind.

- Veritas nondum visibilis.
The truth remains to be seen.

- Salus in numeris donec numerus vester ascendit.
There is safety in numbers until your number is up.

- Numquam nominare inane vacuum.
Never call a void a void.

- Sine pullos nihilum ova.
If there were no chickens there'd be no eggs.

- Ignorantiam didicit.
Ignorance is learned.

- Odium contagiosa est.
Hatred is contagious.

- Maximo sinceritatis ironia.
Irony is the perfection of sincerity.

-

Veritas est scortum sumptuosus.
Truth is a pricey whore.

-

Judaeorum dabo optimus pretium.
Jews will give you the best price.

-

Si videris Judaeus, dicere salve pro me.
If you see a Jew be sure to say I said hello.

-

Omni infringes punctum impotens etiam amare.
Everything breaks at its weakest point including love.

-

Fragilitas solicito amatio.
Fragility is the root of love.

-

Quasi pardus est Judaeus. Sed absque maculis.
A Jew is like a leopard without the spots.

• • •

Caudio Amberian was a Jewish poet and sophist of the first century CE (circa 30–75). He was likely born near Alexandria and spoke or read Aramaic, Hebrew, and Greek. He may have studied with Philo before moving to Rome around 60. In Rome, Amberian started a small school for sophistry, where he engaged students in Socratic-style dialogues. In addition, Amberian was a counselor to Nero in the last years of his reign, following the fire, and he helped set the ground for the move of Josephus and his entourage from Jerusalem to Rome in 71. The only previous translation of Amberian's work, an untitled poem, was published in *Girly Man*.

At his school in Rome, Amberian spoke in a broken or pidgin Latin that some of his students called "barbaric." The only records we have of his writing are the Latin transcriptions made by these notoriously unreliable and sometimes hostile students. The *Amberianum* was reconstructed from shreds and shards at the Sid Caesar Center for Dysraphic Studies. Missing words and the seaming of disconnected parts likely mar the work. The Latin manuscript was discovered on October 4, 1895, buried under a former Minsk dry goods store. The story of the miraculous finding of the *Amberianum* has been told in the award-winning book *The Oy!: How the World Became Pataquerical.*

The reflection precedes the image
Floating midair
Between up and under
Or taking the measure of the sky
Braided coyly with macaroons
That dot the cloudy firmament
Like the last train to Bayonne
Lurches toward Bedlahem
Where the stains are invisible
To everyone but me

for Feng Yi

LAST KIND WORDS

Virtue's a kind
of despair,
masquerading as care.
A bitter
current is for
virtue sweet.
Sublime wine sours
its mouth.
Snakes eat from
its hands.
Jackasses obey its
whim. Self-
nomination papers its
path. Method
is its M.O.,
holding tight to
a higher
love and fervently
displayed empathies.
Virtue's sword
is truth, in
love with
itself, at odds
with others.
Celebrating standards it
fashions, virtue
jams miscreants, shams
malcontents, shaming
those abjure improvement.
The passion
of virtue is
reprimand. Nothing
is more beautiful

to virtue
than compelling justice
and shattering
dissent: slashes in
a pan
that will never
absolve aesthetics.

SHE / MA

Here's real:
Lore our God
Annoyed echo

TURN OFF YOUR POETRY BLOCKER

This is an initial alert. Aesthetic action
Will be taken if there is no response.

Reb couldn't help
smiling when
born-again preach
preached dream of
evangelical heaven,
"bucolic fields, placid
lakes, fruit-punched
valleys"—all that
jazz.

Reb nodded with
demonic glee when
preach preached
dream of Jewish
heaven—"noisy,
smelly, crammed
with bodies jammed
'gainst another,
sardines in cans."

"You know, preach"—
Reb began to speak,
unprompted and
at first in a whisper—
"I dreamed of two
heavens too."

"Jewish heaven is
exactly as in your
dream—a piercing
stench takes time
to bear and an
unceasing cacophony

of argument, shouts,
wails. The place is
filled with all manner
of Jew, observant and
opposed."

Reb's voice began
to rise.

"And not just Jews.
Sunnis and Shia,
Hindus, Catholics,
born-again and
mainline, boisterous,
gesticulating wildly
in streets chock-full
of Buddhists, blasphemers,
unbelievers, even those
never gave belief or
unbelief a plug nickel
of thought."

By now Reb's voice
was echoing, as if
coming from on high.

"In my dream, like yours,
evangelical heaven is
crazy Day-Glo green
fields, pristine vistas that
seem to go to infinity.
Quiet as all get-out.

"For six days and six
nights I wandered through
your heaven, walking in

sublime meadows,
climbing beauteous
mountains, roaming
rolling hills.

"I never felt such peace
in those six days and
those six nights. Nor
such solitude.

"Nobody was there."

No fake verses about what's going on.
No creation or death before poetry.
Compared to which, life's a static sun,
with no heat or illumination.
Affinities, anniversaries, personal anecdotes—don't matter.
No fake poetry with the body,
an excellent, complete and comfortable body—senseless for poetry.

Your spleen, your fits of pleasure or pain in the dark—make no difference.
Don't share with me your feelings,
which reek of equivocation and beat around the bush.
What you think and feel, that is not yet poetry.

No singing about your city—leave it in peace.
Songs aren't machine music or family secrets;
and they're not music heard in passing
nor rumors of the sea on streets lined with spume.

Song's not nature
or community.
Storm and light, fatigue, fright—are of no importance for song.
Poetry—no taking poetry from things!—
elides subject and object.

No dramatizing, no invocations,
no nagging. No wasted time lying.
No belaboring.
Your ivory yacht, your diamond slippers,
your manias and mazurkas, your family skeletons
disappear in time's tunnels, worthless.

No reworking
your buried and melancholy childhood.
No oscillating between mirror and
disappearing memories.
What disappeared wasn't poetry.
What broke was no crystal.

Penetrate, with stealth, words' dominion.
Poems are waiting to be written.
They are paralyzed but without despair.
Calm, fresh, membrane intact.
Mute and brute, immaculate as a dictionary.

Let the poem live within you, then write it.
Be patient with obscurity. Calm down when provoked.
Wait for each poem to become real, consummated
with the power of words
and the power of silence.

No forcing a poem out of limbo.
No picking a lost poem off the floor.
No adulating a poem. Accept it
like it accepts its concrete form concentrated
in space.

Each one
has a thousand secret faces under the surface
that ask you, without interest in the reply—
bad or worse—that you devise:
Did you bring the key?

Notice:
bereft of melody and conceit,
words, still humid, pregnant in sleep,

hide in the night, tumbling in a difficult river
transformed to scorn.

after Carlos Drummond de Andrade's
"Procura da poesia" (1945)
& after John Yau and Michael Palmer

Steve & me &
Andy Lampert
were having this
raucous conversation
at the *Rail*
party a week
back. Steve was
sitting on Phong
& Nathlie's fire
escape at the
edge of that
huge black
steel-grate
terrace, you
know, the kind
you feel
you're just
about to fall
through—
tumbling
fifty
feet
to
the
courtyard
below.
It was the end
of summer &
we gobbled
up the BBQ
dogs with relish
(ugh!). Steve
seemed tired, or

weary, maybe
a bit subdued.
We regaled him
about what folks
nowadays
find funny &
what they don't.
(Don't get me
started!) Steve
taking it all
in with his
curmudgeonly
charm: three
wandering
tummlers, sharing
a moment of
solidarity
in a world
(sooner than
you know)
melts
or turns
ashen.
Steve had
a grace that
refused grace —
& I think he
would've laughed
at the premature
reports of his
death after
his brain
stopped
in its prodigious
tracks while his
body kept on,

giving him a
last dose of
brute life.
I was just
getting to
know him.
—May his memory
be as much
of a Goddamn
blessing as his
presence always
was.

(1946–2019)

sorry to be so sorry
sad to be so sad
distraught at my distress
melancholic on account of my melancholy
depressed to be depressed
anxious about my anxiety
happy to be happy
glad to be glad
disappointed by disappointment
amused to be amused
angry about anger
indifferent to indifference
despairing about despair
lost in my loss
buzzed to be buzzed
dumbfounded to be dumbfounded
hurt by the hurt
wounded by the wound
humiliated by the humiliation
paranoid about paranoia
miffed to be miffed
abject in objectification
unlucky to be unlucky
desiring desire
blankly blank
ashamed to be ashamed
ignorant of my ignorance
guilty feeling guilty
paralyzed by my paralysis
embarrassed by my embarrassment
silenced by my silence
enabled by my immobility
agitated by my agitation

ok being ok
mystified to be confused
inconsolable about being inconsolable
frightened by my fearfulness
encouraged by my timidity

AFTER STEPHEN RATCLIFFE

Horizon line shimmers
At edge of light
Umbra calls echo

    Branch's horizontal intrusion
    Or is it claw?

    Not even quite white or blue
    Turquoise smudge winks

Fading pink fingers of mist
Evanescent liquid dissolving
Moment of change

There was a young lady from New York
Who dined each night on stewed pork.
One day she went hunting
For pumpkins in the ocean
That silly young lady from New York.

COVIDITY

The covid gonna get me
If not now, it will
The covid gonna kill me
Find me where I live

Buried under covers
Sheltered in the hall
Trading goodbyes to all my friends
Through goddamn 15-foot walls

The covid'll get me
Get me bad
My lungs are weak
And I am much misunderstood

I practice social distance
Even got an oversize mask
Feel like the Lone Ranger
Just before he got the clap

The covid going to find me
If not today, in time
The covid after me
Find exactly where I am

Call it social distance
I call it pain in the soul
You say I can handle it
But it's too heavy a load

The covid 'round the corner
'll thrash me till I blue

But that's not my worry
Terrified for you

You've always been distant
But not from me
Now I feel you drifting
Like you're far out at sea

The covid gonna get me
If not now any day
The covid got my number
Knows just where I stay

You say I'll manage social distance
That I can make it work
But if I'm distant from you
I'm sunk before I swum

The covid gonna get me
If not now, soon
The covid has me up all night
Fighting 'gainst all this gloom

Too much death surrounding
I darn near given up
Keep calling on the telephone
But you're hung up on Skype

The covid coming
Sure to get us good
Our lungs are weak
And we are much misunderstood

23

You are my shepherd.
I shall not want.
You lead me from dark, turbulent waters
To sun-drenched meadows.
You bring my life back to me
Leading me on paths of splendor.
Though I walk in the shadows of death
Sick with fears, grief, and uncertainties
I know you are with me.
Your memory consoles.
You set out a feast before me
Softening, with care, life's blows
So that now my cup overflows.
Let kindness and truthfulness take hold of me
All the days of my life.
I shall dwell in your house
Forever.

Refugees are
at home in
their pilgrimage,
the landed
deluded
in the narcotic
of possession:
values
found in
passing, in
the occlusion
of
prospect and
deferral. These
veils
bare
the weight of
significance
while meaning
fills the
pores
of a
holiness
foundering
in its
refusal
to
name. To
be
foreign
to
oneself
and familiar

to each
other
is more
grace
than any
one
of us
deserves
and
as
elusive
as the
holes
that pock-
mark
the whole
God-damn
confab.

for Hank Lazer

sometimes a bee's just a bee
and a sting just a sting
and song just a song
and sorrow just sorrow
sometimes the blue just gets to you
and the black an instrument
of form's indelible intransigence

drawing by Amy Sillman

*Key: A Aries, T Taurus, G Gemini, C Cancer, L Leo, V Virgo, Li Libra,
S Scorpio, Sa Sagittarius, Ca Capricorn, Aq Aquarius, P Pisces. Each
section covers one year, then rotates. Add 12 to each year to get dates after
2030, so "2019" extends to 2031, 2045, etc.*

A2019, T2020, G2021, C2022, L2023, V2024, Li2025, S2026, Sa2027,
Ca2028, Aq2029, P2030
Anticipated reversals occur in unanticipated locations: avoid planar sur-
faces. As Saturn and Pluto come into alignment, prepare for irrepress-
ible nostalgia. Casual attachments provide a medley of diversions from
long-term fantasies. Mix of sulfur and magnesium is at its height on the
12th and 29th: stay clear of disarticulating headwinds while remaining
open to miscalibrated address. Seek pine- and coconut-flavored dishes.
Preferred alcohol: Anisette (neat).

T19, G20, C21, L22, V23, Li24, S25, Sa26, Ca27, Aq28, P29, A30
Reach out to long-estranged family members to say *life is better without
you*. Don't back away from regrets. Outer Andromeda is fragmenting
into deep time shallows: time to stop the ambivalence and say *no*. Mid-
month is best time for buying short but avoid other financial transac-
tions. Look over your back before making sudden move. Avoid disco.
Linger in crinoline. Seek wool products and avoid rayon. Preferred
alcohol: Pisco (sour).

G19, C20, L21, V22, Li23, S24, Sa25, Ca26, Aq27, P28, A29, T30
Pegasus wars with Orion, but zones of calm when Pyxis is rising. Smells
intensify in arboreal regions. Old lovers come to mind, posing immedi-
ate threat. Keep eyes on interstitial aggravations. Turmeric and clove in
seventh and thirteenth weeks will ward off transvirtual infection. Travel
southward when possible but not before 6am local time. Persons from
Uruguay will offer gift: not necessary to return favor but wait one week
before opening. Seek volcanic dust. Preferred alcohol: Koskenkorva
(with bitters).

<u>C19, L20, V21, Li22, S23, Sa24, Ca25, Aq26, P27, A28, T29, G30</u>
Turbulence in the nebula. Dark Matter in retrovariance. Take only
third offers. Dress in chartreuse on even-numbered days and in mute
orchid on odd days. Friendships cement in near term on days with "3"
(3, 13, 30, 31) but stay at sea level on days with "5" (5, 15). Your horse
will "place" on "0" days (10, 20, 30). Moods conform with waning
and waxing moon, great calm at new moon. Avoid sexual contact
at full moon. Seek bougainvillea. Preferred alcohol: Slivovitz (with
orange peel).

<u>L19, V20, Li21, S22, Sa23, Ca24, Aq25, P26, A27, T28, G29, C30</u>
Turn no one away. Gold is buried just beyond shoreline. Emotional
tides are uneven, but stay with them or undercurrent will pull you
down. Magnetic fields from the melting polar caps run roughshod over
love life. Avoid newspapers in second weeks; at other times start with
recipes, when available. Jupiter crosses Saturn in perfect Equinity Sem-
blance: keep measured distance from newcomers. Saturn is lodestar
whose course tracks in avoirdupois: pound for feckless, dram for egress,
stone for gravitation. Seek cantilevers. Preferred alcohol: Aguardiente
(over ice).

<u>V19, Li20, S21, Sa22, Ca23, Aq24, P25, A26, T27, G28, C29, L30</u>
"The seraph / Is satyr in Saturn, according to his thoughts" (Wallace
Stevens). Close call becomes near miss. Bounty holds only when seared.
Jade is talisman of recusal and redaction. Aspiration punctuates lunar
flares. Retreat in hollow days, parry on pivots. "The genius of misfor-
tune / Is not a sentimentalist": defy writ to rend. The tally is incendiary,
but fortune comes in buckets. Disable charms to charm. The following
day rips away the scuff of last. Cleave to presenting, adjacent insistence
deems purpose. Seek such sentiment (not sentimental). Preferred alco-
hol: Drambuie (splits).

<u>Li19, S20, Sa21, Ca22, Aq23, P24, A25, T26, G27, C28, L29, V30</u>
Cold mouth, hot lips. Perpetuate fevered state, outlives livid transien-
cies. Dig hard but cede ground. Solar flares quash unspoken dreams but
open path for development. Meteor showers in the south inflate cur-

rency. Lucky numbers: 8, 13, 331. Orient Eastward for repose, Westward for reflection. Scent: basil. Keep cool, under 60 degrees F, on first and last days of every month except first and last months. Eat soup weekly, alternating hot and cold. Seek predisposition. Preferred alcohol: moonshine (with rum).

S19, Sa20, Ca21, Aq22, P23, A24, T25, G26, C27, L28, V29, Li30
Watch for mid-Pacific squalls. Stay totally clear on such days. Even the smallest thought can betray you. Confide only in friends from past five years and only about matters that occurred over that time. Signs of incompatibility include swift and frequent eyelid clatter, extravagant hand motion, and midday drowsiness. Signs of compatibility include sudden rain, heightened gait, and tender elbow. High risk of falling into dark matter. Vigilance pays off on 3rd, 12th, and 19th day. Seek vermillion. Preferred alcohol: Trappist brandy (spritz).

Sa19, Ca20, Aq21, P22, A23, T24, G25, C26, L27, V28, Li29, S30
"What is most full seems empty. Yet its use will never fail. What is most straight seems bent. The greatest skill seems like clumsiness. The greatest eloquence like stuttering" (*Tao Te Ching*). Climb to the tallest point within your reach, then lie flat at the lowest point, saying these words. Saturn's rings surround your despair: have courage! Sing a song of childhood when you feel farthest from it. Every crack of thunder speaks with the voice of your dearest lost loves. Seek oak. Preferred alcohol: rice wine (chilled).

Ca19, Aq20, P21, A22, T23, G24, C25, L26, V27, Li28, S29, Sa30
Settled matters unravel: time to take the advantage. Tropical depressions complicate unfamiliar liaisons, providing opportunities for needed adventure. Catch a falling star and put it in your pocket. Uranus rising: auspicious for small-bore improvements but not major renovation. Act as if "there is no use in a center" (Stein): galvanize desire against regret and regret against compulsory well-being. Bird song provides big tip on holiday parties. Seek negative velocity. Preferred alcohol: mescal (with lemon).

Aq19, P20, A21, T22, G23, C24, L25, V26, Li27, S28, Sa29, Ca30
Sharp descent of Calypso Cluster drags Marmolean Veil into direct imbrication. Lucky numbers −6, −18, −871. Lucky colors: maroon, dead-island blue, mustard gray. Stay pressurized: do not leave capsule. Pseudoglossia is music from outer spheres but do not interpret or translate. Live in, not for, the moment. Seal the deal (resistance is a form of divination). Seek adjacency. Preferred alcohol: Cachaça (with lime and sugar).

P219, A20, T21, G22, C23, L24, V25, Li26, S27, Sa28, Ca29, Aq30
Let envy propel you to eternity. Otherwise, duck and cover. Orion lays bare prognosis: structure treatment in response. Anxiety cools to fermenting antagonism: perpetuate memorialization. Sylvan linings pocket outsize payouts. Scatter in flutter, halt, then heave hard. Use thyme and ginger on 6th and 8th days of month, otherwise paprika (except on first and last days). Time will stand still at last moment. Follow the radiant sound of whoosh and whap. Declare insolvency as metaphysical foundation: blur affinities and self-identifications. Midmonths probe deep into shadows: reject false bottoms. Seek inardency. Preferred alcohol: Absinthe (with Bénédictine).

A flailing poet came to the Alter Cocker Rebbe for advice on how to improve his art. "Stop cursing God," Rebbe said defiantly. "I constantly praise God in my poems," insisted the poet. "Stop disparaging your fellow man!" said the rabbi, his voice suffused with sorrow, contempt, and world-weariness. "My poems are filled with praise for my fellow human beings," the poet lamented, his head deeply bowed. "Show some respect for the nonhuman world," the Rebbe, now agitated, shouted. "My work is second to none in its engagement with nature," the poor poet pleaded. "I am sorry," the Alter Cocker Rebbe told the poet. "There is no help. You are like a sinking ship with nothing to throw off."

after Mark Twain

THE DEATH OF SEAN BONNEY

In-
c-
an-
de-
scent
co-
met-
s
doubl-
e cross
night
sky,
blood-
ied, bow-
leg,
raging '-
gainst
th-
e machi-
ne of
our liv-
es as
i-
f
liver
were
Blake's
s-
word
& ly-
ric
e-
nun-

c-
iatio-
n
de-
mol-
i-
sh
tap-
es-
tries
of
fei-
g-
ne-
d
ac-
com-
mo-
datio-
n.
I
nev-
er
cou-
ld be
tha-
t,
dri-
fting
dow-
nwin-
d, tru-
st-
ing no-
thi-
ng but

dark fl-
ash
of fu-
til-
e fis-
sures.
D-
eath
bein-
g an
e-
vent
not
of th-
is
worl-
d bu-
t c-
om-
ing:
qui-
x-
o-
ti-
c,
i-
m-
mo-
bi-
l-
e,
free.

(November 20, 2019)

Taste is not so much
A matter of opinion
As a thorn cleaving my
Tongue, from which I,
Automatic, conjure
Twin thin rings, interpapillary
Bouquets of cloven
Misfortune, abutting
Caulk cabins in deciduous
Rows. Mired in matter, it's
Only moments to take off,
Who, in a parallel reality,
Paddles along with nickels
To burn. If I can't convince
You of that, what's the point
Of trying?

TURNKEY

In the dark world of me and you
In a mirror enduring forever
My breathing, my heat
Sealed in a text
Unreadable long since

BEFORE THE PROMISE

I drew a blank on a torn door
Drew another, then no more
Got stung, pedaled frowns
Knew things was bust
(No way outta town)

Sometimes it done it its way
Then again, harder to say—
What's looking up
Decides to knock you down

Before the promise of tomorrow
Tomorrow came

Morning on this pole
Midnight at the other
Slipping, slapping, sliding
On a cockamamie roll

Yesterday's dreams dissolve
Into today's goodbyes
I set out on a camel's hump
Came back with just the eyes

Before the promise of tomorrow
Tomorrow came

A farther distance that we go
Within each moment spent
Then ever's sent by Heaven
Or scaled by human ken

Before the promise of tomorrow
Tomorrow came

We twist, we turn
Undo ourselves in tripled throws
My goodness, how the time has passed!—
Let's get our stuff and beat a path

To what we never knew
Nor will, nor who, nor say

Before the promise of tomorrow
Tomorrow came

for the 2020 class
Phi Beta Kappa of Eta
(Ohio Wesleyan University)

VEYISKADASH
[MOURNER'S KADDISH]

let the memory
of the dead
be sanctified
even as flesh
decays
spirit stays
in memory
is body, soul
what's left
is loss
outlasts life
good, bad
rights, wrong
love, anger,
hopes, disappointment
care, neglect, communions and
disunion, sorrows, joy
the life lived
now holy
in memory
in tears in bitterness
gratitude delight
let the names of the dead
be exalted
& so may
[names of the those mourned]
be praised
honored, extolled
glorified, adored
beyond earthly cares
or songs of comfort

beyond blame or merit
let there now be
acknowledgment
in this transition
beyond blessing

Death is the end of all sadness
Storm follows each moment of bliss
Here lies the road to true madness
Deeper than locks in abyss
Storm echoes surfeit of gladness
Loneliness lives by its wits

SONG SPARROW

Maids, maids, maids
Put on your tea
Kettle, kettle, kettle.
No time to waste
Get out your bass
Fiddle, fiddle, fiddle.
Young lads make haste
Dance to your love's
Riddle, riddle, riddle.

If anything I have done
Cancels what I feel
Then put me on a boat
Without a keel
And I will row my way back to you
Whatever else I do
Whatever else I do

Some of these poems originally appeared in *The A-Line, Arts & Letters, Australian Book Review, Berkeley Poetry Review, b2o (boundary 2 online), Blazing Stadium, Boston Compass, Brooklyn Rail, Caliban, Conjunctions, Chicago Review, CCAR Journal: The Reform Jewish Quarterly, Critical Inquiry, Equalizer, Frieze, Have Your Chill, Journal of Writing in Creative Practice, Lingo, Mandorla, Manor House Quarterly, n/a, Ocean State Review, On and On Screen, Pangyrus, Paris Review, PN Review, Poems in the Aftermath* (Indolent Books), *PoetsArtists, Politics and Letters, Pratik, Przekroj, Salmagundi, Slope, Table Talk, Veer Journal,* and *Wave Composition.* And in the liner notes for *Winged Serpents: Six Encomiums for Cecil Taylor* (Tzadik, 2018) and Nicolas Hodges's *Complete Piano Works of Brian Ferneyhough* (Neos, 2015).

Epigraph: my transcription of 1930 vocal recording by Geeshie Wiley.

"Reading Red Redux": In 1998, Walther König (Cologne) published *Reading Red* with my poems superimposed on twenty-five of the images in Richard Tuttle's series "New Mexico–New York." Those poems were published, without images, in *Girly Man.* A special edition of the König book was made with additions by Tuttle along with these twenty-five poems.

"Boat Ride on West Lake (Pastoral)": Nie Niezhenzhao asked me to write for an anthology of poems by foreigners on Hangzhou's iconic West Lake. Williams's "Pastoral" came to mind.

"Nuclear Blanks": Homophonic translations of four poems by Esteban Pujals Gesalí: "Eucaristía," "Autorretratorrobot," "Nunca lo suficientemente" and "Hay quien me apuñalaría," from *Blanco Nuclear* (Málaga: Puerta del Mar, 1985).

"On the Line": Written for *A Broken Thing: Poets on the Line*, ed. Emily Rosko and Anton Vander Zee (Iowa City: University of Iowa Press, 2011).

"Look for the Address": Ted Greenwald did a series of interviews for the *Poetry Project Newsletter*. This one was published in April / May 1988 issue.

"Echologs": "Echologs" is by Bernstein, based on Richard Tuttle's initial translation and ongoing conversation. First published on the covers of his *You Never See the Same Color Twice* (Cologne: Getty Research Institute and Walther König, 2017). A pamphlet of our translation, together with a set of earlier translations, was published by Arts & Letters in 2020.

"Poetic Citizenship and Negative Dialectics": Presented at the Center for Humanities, CUNY Graduate Center, on November 16, 2017, as part of a forum, organized by Kyoo Lee, called "Poetics Citizenship Today.MP3" and first published in *The A-Line*.

"Swan Songs": Written for a festschrift for Richard Sieburth and included in *Ezra's Book: Poetry from the Ezra Pound International Conference* (Clemson, SC: Clemson University Press, 2019).

"Amberianum": First published as a pamphlet by No Press (Calgary, 2016) and collected in *Transpoetic Exchange: Haroldo de Campos, Octavio Paz, and Other Multiversal Dialogues* (Lewisburg, PA: Bucknell University Press, 2020), with excerpts in *Short Circuits: Aphorisms, Fragments, and Literary Anomalies* (Tucson: Schaffner Press, 2018).

"Duplexities": From a series of over one hundred works made in collaboration with Amy Sillman in 2011. Sillman made the drawings on an iPhone with her pinky. Image used with the permission of the artist.

INDEX